Hydropower

Hydropower

Christopher Bahn

Living in THE FUTURE

CREATIVE EDUCATION

CREATIVE PAPERBACKS

Published by Creative Education and Creative Paperbacks
P.O. Box 227, Mankato, Minnesota 56002
Creative Education and Creative Paperbacks are imprints of The Creative Company
www.thecreativecompany.us

Book design by Blue Design (www.bluedes.com)
Art direction by Graham Morgan
Edited by Barbara Ciletti

Photographs by Getty Images/Bob Rowan, 29, Minnesota Historical Society, 23, Wang Huifu/VCG, 30; Pexels/Alan Kabeš, 37, Gül Işık, 10, Pixabay, 9, Sergey Pesterev, 42; Shutterstock/Planton Anton, 17, Uncle_Dave, 44; Unsplash/American Public Power Association, cover, Dan Meyers, 2, Gabor Koszegi, 14, Kees Streefkerk, 4–5, Manny Becerra, cover, Tyke Jones, 34; Wikimedia Commons/GlacierNPS, 45, H. Zell, 6–7, MasaneMiyaPA, 26, P, Hughes, 13, Patrick McCully, 25, public domain, 20, Tavasoli mohsen, 19, Tswgb, 41, U.S. Bureau of Reclamation, 33, Vitafougue, 38

Every effort has been made to contact copyright holders for material reproduced in this book. Any omissions will be rectified in subsequent printings if notice is given to the publisher.

Library of Congress Cataloging-in-Publication Data
Names: Bahn, Christopher (Children's story writer) author
Title: Hydropower / Christopher Bahn.
Description: Mankato, Minnesota : Creative Education and Creative Paperbacks, [2026] | Series: Living in the future | Includes bibliographical references and index. | Audience: Ages 10-14 | Audience: Grades 7-9 | Summary: "A dive into the science of using water to generate electricity. It explains how hydropower plants work and their potential in providing clean, renewable energy for communities around the world. Written for middle-grade readers, it includes real-life examples of energy use, sidebars, a glossary, and an index"— Provided by publisher.
Identifiers: LCCN 2025015986 (print) | LCCN 2025015987 (ebook) | ISBN 9798895811221 library binding | ISBN 9798896800750 paperback | ISBN 9798895812488 ebook
Subjects: LCSH: Water-power—Juvenile literature | Dams—Design and construction— Juvenile literature
Classification: LCC TC146 .B34 2026 (print) | LCC TC146 (ebook)
LC record available at https://lccn.loc.gov/2025015986
LC ebook record available at https://lccn.loc.gov/2025015987

Printed in the United States

CONTENTS

The Force of Water

Water is one of the most powerful and dynamic forces on Earth. Over centuries, mighty rivers carved massive canyons and reshaped entire landscapes, while devastating tsunamis and floods have wrought terrible destruction in just minutes. On the day after Christmas in 2004, a massive earthquake struck the coast of the Indonesian island of Sumatra in the Indian Ocean. The quake itself was not very deadly despite its colossal magnitude. It happened deep in the ocean and away from populated areas. However, it did unleash a deadly tsunami—a massive wall of water that reached 30 meters (100 feet) at its maximum height. This wave triggered massive devastation not only in Indonesia but countries hundreds of miles away. More than 200,00 people lost their lives.

But as with fire and nuclear energy, humans have learned to harness this awe-inspiring power of water to do good. Today, **hydropower** provides water and electricity to power our civilizations, generating about 17 percent of the world's electricity.

Pitlochry Dam in Scotland is one of nine stations in the Tummel Valley hydroelectric scheme.

CHAPTER 1:

How It Works

Energy is central to human civilization. Modern society requires large amounts of energy to function, and we have built enormous, complex systems to generate and distribute that energy. Continent-spanning networks of power lines connect our cities, homes, hospitals, and schools.

Thousands of miles of roads carry millions of cars and trucks. Trains, airplanes and cargo ships crisscross the world. Our energy network runs largely on **fossil fuels** such as coal, oil, and gas. But these fuels are expensive, polluting, and contribute to **global warming**—and they will eventually be used up. It is increasingly important to find **renewable** and **sustainable** alternative energy sources, including solar, wind, geothermal, nuclear power, biofuels, and the topic of this book, hydropower.

Water is a vital natural resource. All life on Earth depends on it, and our own bodies are made up of 70 percent water. It also covers some two-thirds of the surface of the Earth. It creates the rain and lakes and rivers that shape the landscape. And for thousands of years, humans have used the endless **flow** of that water to power civilization. Today, hydropower provides about 17 percent of all electricity made in the world— making it one of the world's most important alternative energy sources. along with solar and wind power

ater is about 800 times denser than air,. This makes it much heavier, with greater force and energy when it moves. Devices like **dams** and **waterwheels** have allowed humans to redirect water from rivers and streams for farming and other purposes. Hydropower was one of the first methods used to generate electricity, giving rise to the continent-spanning power line grids that connect our cities and make modern civilization possible. It's still one of the main methods of making electricity, though far outweighed by fossil fuels.

There are three main types of hydropower systems: **reservoir** dams, run-of-river systems, and pumped storage dams. Reservoir dams are the most common. A dam blocks a river, creating a large lake behind it. Water is released through controlled channels, turning turbines that generate electricity. The farther the water falls, the more power it creates. Some dams are huge, like the Hoover Dam on the Colorado River. It is 726 feet tall and provides water for 20 million people while generating 2,000 megawatts of electricity. Yet, most hydropower dams are much smaller, producing around 55

Hoover Dam on the Colorado River is an example of a reservoir dam.

ZOOM IN: HEADS UP

To find the ideal location for a hydropower dam across a river, engineers look for sites where the amount of energy that can be drawn from the force of the water is maximized. This is measured by concepts known as "head" and "flow." Flow measures how much water goes through the dam over a given time. Head is determined by elevation, or the height difference between where the water enters the hydro facility and where it leaves to return the river. A higher head increases water pressure, or the force of the flow. This is why the most powerful hydropower dams are so large: The bigger the fall, the more power can be generated.

megawatts each. Run-of-river systems don't always need a dam. Instead, they use turbines placed directly in the river or water channeled from the river. These systems are less harmful to the environment because they don't flood land to make a reservoir. But they also can't store water for later use because they depend on the river's natural flow, which changes with the seasons. One of the largest run-of-river projects is the Belo Monte Dam in Brazil, which produces 11.2 gigawatts of electricity. Pumped storage dams work like a giant battery. When energy demand is low, water is pumped back to the upper reservoir. Then, when demand rises, operators release the water to generate power. This system helps keep electricity available when needed most. Such dams are widely used in places like Washington, California, and Oregon.

Most hydropower comes from rivers, but the ocean has even more potential energy. The sea covers 70% of Earth's surface, and waves and tides can also provide power. Ocean power is still being tested because it's costly and hard to build machines that can handle rough saltwater.

Hydropower is a low-cost way to make electricity. After they're built, hydropower plants are cheap to run, can last up to 100 years, and create very little pollution. In Iceland, almost all electricity comes from hydropower and geothermal energy, making it one of the cleanest energy producers in the world. Hydropower is also very efficient—about 90% of the energy in flowing water is turned into electricity, while fossil fuel plants only reach about 50%.

Even though hydropower is a renewable energy source, it has drawbacks. Large dams can harm local ecosystems and force people to move. According to environmental research, dam construction has displaced between 30 to 60 million people throughout history. The worst-case scenario is a dam failure. If a dam collapses, it can unleash deadly floods. One of the biggest disasters was the Banqiao Dam failure in China in 1975, which killed 240,000 people. This tragedy showed the dangers of poorly designed infrastructure.

Despite these challenges, hydropower remains an important part of the world's energy future. It is a clean, reliable, and renewable energy source that helps reduce reliance on fossil fuels. Scientists and engineers continue to improve hydropower technology to make it more sustainable and less harmful to the environment.

ZOOM IN: SPIN CYCLES

Hydropower gets its energy from sunlight and gravity through a process called the water cycle. sunlight turns ocean water into clouds, forming vapor. Wind moves the clouds over land, where they drop rain. Gravity pulls rain down rivers and back to the ocean, and the cycle repeats. Because this cycle never stops, hydropower is renewable like wind and solar power.

The water you're drinking right now might be billions of years old and all because of the water cycle!

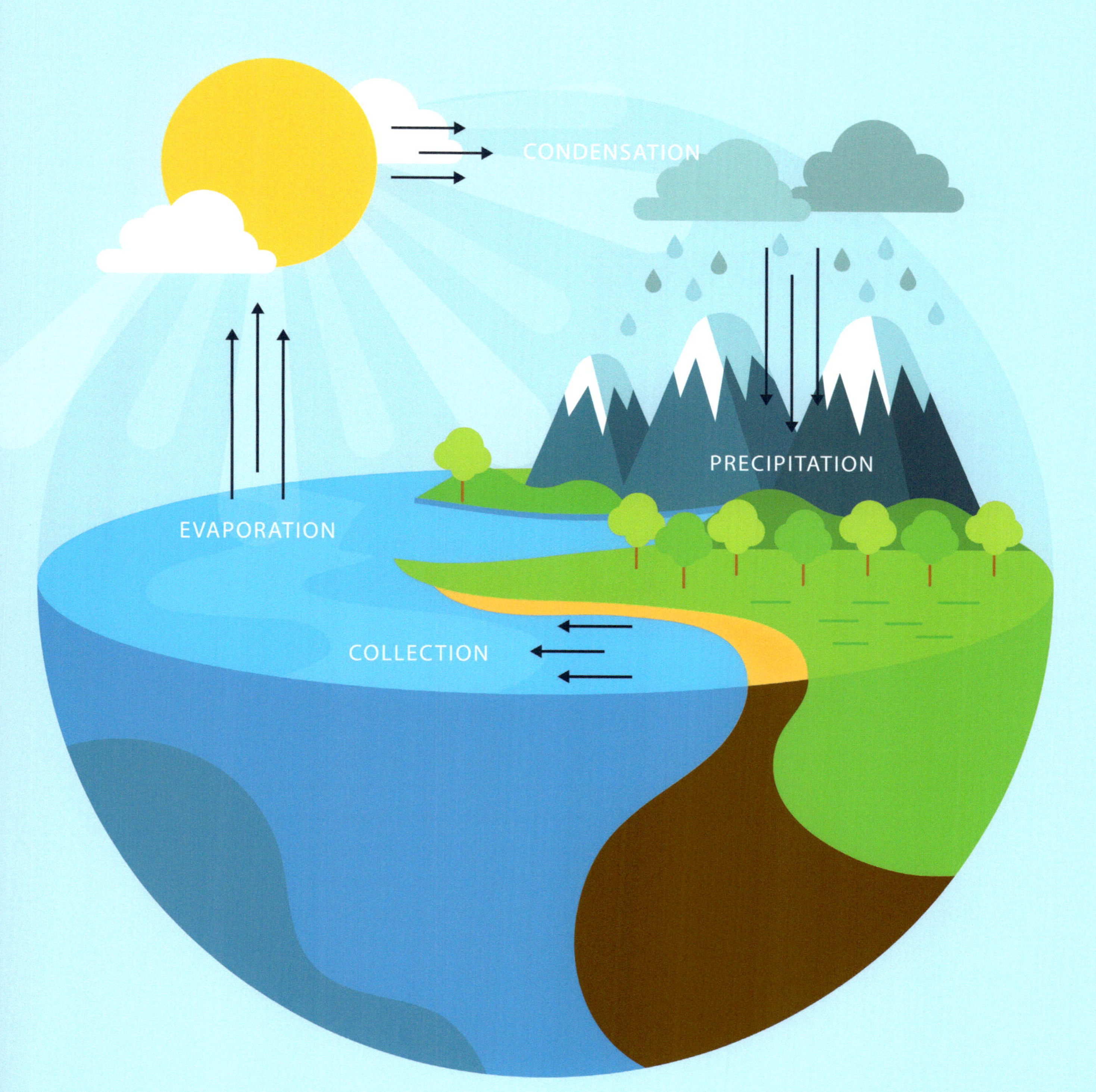
CONDENSATION
PRECIPITATION
EVAPORATION
COLLECTION

One of the longest qanats, located in Gonabad, Iran, stretches an impressive 70 kilometers and is still in use today.

CHAPTER 2:

History of Hydropower

People have used flowing water for power for thousands of years. **Irrigation** was one of the first ways people used water power, by digging canals to move river water for farming and drinking. Around 550 B.C.E., the Achaemenid Empire in Persia built what may have been the first major water system. They created dams, canals, and underground tunnels called qanats to bring water to cities and farms.

Then during late 2nd centruy B.C.E., the ancient Egyptians used **hydraulic** power in a device now called the Archimedes screw, named after the Greek mathematician who described it in 234 B.C.E. This tool lifted water from low areas for irrigation and powered mills. Today, modern versions can even create electricity.

In China, during the Han Dynasty, inventors turned their attention to waterwheels. These machines powered tools for making iron, grinding grain,

Water-Lifting Wheel on the Huang He river in 1875.

ZOOM IN: A LONG LEGACY

The first big hydroelectric plant in the U.S. was built at Niagara Falls, New York. It was designed by Nikola Tesla and George Westinghouse and opened in 1895. It sent electricity to New York City 400 miles away!

and producing paper. The idea spread and may have been developed separately in Egypt and Greece. Some waterwheels looked like Ferris wheels that utilized gravity to lift water by filling buckets at the bottom. They would rise as the wheel turned and be emptied at the top. Others were built in fast-moving streams to spin horizontally. By the second century C.E., Romans in Gaul (now France) built a factory with 16 water-powered mills. By 1086 C.E., waterwheels were common across Europe, with at least 5,624 recorded in England alone. By the 12th century, European monks were using them to make metal tools and olive oil.

During the Industrial Revolution in the 1700s and 1800s, machines changed the world, and water played a big role. Although coal later became the main energy source of this time-period, waterpower helped start it all. By 1747, American settlers had built 90 water-powered sawmills in New England, fueling the shipbuilding industry. In 1771, English factory owner Richard Arkwright used waterwheels to run machines in one of the world's first large textile factories.

The use of hydropower for electricity began in the mid-1700s. French engineer Bernard Forest de Bélidor studied modern water power in his book *Architecture Hydraulique*. In 1827, another French inventor, Bernard Fourneyron, created the first modern water turbine. His design forced water through a tube, increasing its speed and pressure to spin blades and produce power. British–American engineer James Francis later improved this idea, creating the Francis turbine, which is still widely used today.

In the 1800s, hydropower boosted textile production and milling. In Minneapolis, water from the Mississippi River's St. Anthony Falls powered the world's largest flour mill. As the 20th century began, hydroelectricity became more common, helping industries and cities grow. The first major hydroelectric dam was built in 1882 on the Fox River in Appleton, Wisconsin. It powered a paper mill and the home of its owner, H.F. Rogers. Within five years, there were 40 to 50 hydroelectric plants in the U.S. and Canada. By 1899, that number had grown to 500, and the technology had spread to Australia, Germany, and China.

Today, hydropower provides about one-sixth of the world's electricity. A key development was pumped storage, which was created in Italy and Switzerland. This method stores water for later use, allowing power to be generated when needed. The idea spread to the U.S. by 1930, improving the flexibility of hydroelectric plants.

In the early 1900s, the U.S. led the world in building large dams. President Franklin Roosevelt's Rural Electrification Act of 1936 expanded the country's electrical grid, with a strong focus on hydropower. Many dams were built, especially in the Pacific Northwest and Tennessee Valley. The biggest was the Hoover Dam, finished in 1936. At the time, it was the largest hydroelectric dam in the world, producing 1,345 megawatts of electricity. Today, the largest in the

St. Anthony Falls played a vital role in powering Minneapolis's flour milling industry, earning the city the nickname 'Flour Milling Capital of the World' from 1880 to 1930.

INTERNATIONAL STOCK FOOD FACTO
PILLSBURY A MILL, LARGEST FLOUR MILL IN THE WORLD.
35,000

U.S. is the Grand Coulee Dam in Washington state, which produces 6,800 megawatts.

Hydropower was the first widely used renewable energy, fueling the 19th-century Industrial Revolution and powering early electric grids. The others, like wind, solar, geothermal and biofuels, did not really catch up until major investment in their development happened after the energy crisis of the 1970s.

As other forms have matured, hydropower as a percentage of all forms of renewable energy has actually decreased, dropping from 45 percent in 2005 to 31 in 2021. But that drop also has to do with increased drought in the western U.S., and the controversial nature of hydropower. Environmental groups like the Nature Conservancy and Sierra Club have actively opposed the building of new dams, which disrupt rivers' natural movement of soil and the life cycles of the animals who live in them, such as salmon. There are human costs as well: Entire towns have had to move when dams are built, because the reservoir behind the dam turns the land into a lake. New dam construction in America has, for the most part, stopped, due to these concerns. In 1940, hydropower provided 40% of U.S. electricity. Today,

ZOOM IN: MOVING THE PHARAOHS

When Egypt built the Aswan Dam on the Nile River in the mid-1900s, it helped control floods and produced hydropower. But there was a big problem—it flooded 22 ancient sites, including the famous Abu Simbel temple with its massive stone statues of Pharaoh Ramesses II. Egypt immediately launched a rescue mission. The effort took 12 years and the help of 40 countries to save the 3,000-year-old treasures for future generations.

The Klamath River dams were removed in 2024, marking the largest dam removal project in U.S. history. This effort restored approximately 400 miles of free-flowing river, significantly benefiting local ecosystems.

it supplies between 6% and 10%, depending on rainfall and water levels. While its role has decreased, hydropower remains an important renewable energy source. Scientists continue to improve hydroelectric technology, balancing energy needs with environmental protection.

CHAPTER 3:

Hydropower Today

The United States is still a major player in hydropower, but other countries have taken the lead in building new dams over the last 20 years.

By 1965, North America was the top hydropower region, with the U.S. and Canada constructing huge projects like Hoover Dam and Niagara Falls power plants. But by 2023, the Asia-Pacific region had pulled far ahead. Today, the world's biggest hydropower producers are, in order, China, Brazil, Canada, the U.S., and Russia. Of the 30 largest hydroelectric dams worldwide, China has 13, while Brazil has seven.

Even with the rise of other energy sources, hydropower remains an important part of the U.S. energy system. It provides steady electricity and helps reduce carbon emissions. In 2023, hydropower made up about 5.6% of total U.S. electricity. In the Pacific Northwest, especially in Oregon and Washington, it produces around 70% of the region's power. Every state in the U.S. uses at least some hydropower. The magazine *International Water Power* reported in 2024 that spending on U.S. hydropower dams and reservoirs grew from $200 million in

The Xin'anjiang Hydropower Station, completed in 1960, was China's first large-scale hydroelectric power project designed and constructed independently.

ZOOM IN: STAIRWAYS FOR SALMON

One major problem with river dams is that they block fish from migrating upstream to spawn. Species like salmon, eels, and sturgeon rely on this journey to lay their eggs, and without access, their numbers can decline.

One solution: fish ladders. These structures aren't ladders in the usual sense—fish don't have hands, after all. Instead, they're a series of connected pools that fish leap through, step by step, to bypass the dam.

2004 to $2 billion today. Most of this money goes toward fixing and upgrading old dams, along with some new projects.

Hydropower depends on geography, since it works best where there are big rivers and and mountainous regions with steep drops in elevation. In some places, it is just one part of a larger energy system. In dry areas like North Africa and Australia, there isn't enough water to make hydropower practical. Even where hydropower works well, it changes with the seasons. In the U.S., hydropower production is highest in April and May, when melting snow swells rivers. It is lowest in October when water levels drop.

Hydropower is extemely effective in locations with the right conditions. Norway, with its many mountains and rivers, gets about 88% of its electricity from hydro, with most of the rest from wind power. This gives Norway the highest share of renewable energy in Europe and some of the lowest emissions. In Iceland, more than two-thirds of electricity comes from hydropower, with the rest from geothermal energy. Across the European Union, hydropower is the second-largest renewable electricity source, behind

Fish ladders, also known as fishways, allow fish to "climb" over obstacles like dams or waterfalls during migration.

The massive Three Gorges Dam has slightly altered the Earth's rotation!

wind power and just ahead of solar. A 2022 report from the European Commission said that hydropower made up nearly 30% of the EU's renewable electricity and about 12.3% of its total electricity when fossil fuels were included.

No country has expanded hydropower faster than China. In 2008, hydropower made up 8% of China's electricity. Since then, that number has more than doubled. China now produces nearly three times as much hydroelectricity as Brazil, the second-largest producer. Most of China's hydro development is along the Yangtze River, which flows from the mountains of Tibet. The largest of these projects is the Three Gorges Dam, which became the world's biggest hydropower dam when it was completed in 2012. It produces 22,500 megawatts of electricity—16 times more than the Hoover Dam. The dam stretches 1.4 miles (2.3 kilometers) wide and stands 607 feet (185 meters) tall. The reservoir behind it covers about 1,000 square kilometers. It generates enough power for 60 million homes in China. However, building the dam forced 1.2 million people to relocate and may have contributed to the extinction of the Chinese river dolphin. China also leads in pumped-storage dams, including the Fengning plant, which became the world's biggest in 2024 at 3.6 gigawatts. The second-largest pumped-storage facility, at 3 gigawatts, is in Bath County, Virginia.

South America's massive rivers make it another major hydropower region. Brazil, Peru, Ecuador, and Colombia all rely heavily on hydro. In the 1990s, Brazil built enough dams on the Amazon River to generate 90% of its electricity. Yet long droughts made the government reconsider relying so much on hydropower. Even now, Brazil's electricity is mostly hydroelectric, with biofuels as the second-largest source. While the Amazon River is huge, much of it is too flat for effective dam-building. Instead, Brazil's largest dam, Itaipu, sits on the Paraná River along the border with Paraguay. It produces 14 gigawatts of electricity, supplying about 90% of Paraguay's power and 10% of Brazil's. The Itaipu project, like many other dams, was controversial because it flooded Guaíra Falls, once the world's largest waterfall by volume.

Hydropower in South America is expected to grow in the coming decades. Countries like Peru, Bolivia, and Ecuador are shifting away from fossil fuels and investing more in renewable energy. With vast river systems, these nations have the potential to generate even more hydroelectricity in the future.

ZOOM IN: A GRAND DAM

The northwestern U.S. is great for hydropower because it has fast rivers and tall mountains. In Washington, Oregon, and northern California, over half of the electricity comes from hydropower. The Grand Coulee Dam, the largest in the nation, spans the Columbia River in Washington. It's one of the largest dams in the world and can make 6,800 megawatts of power—enough to run a million trains!

The Grand Coulee Dam
contains enough concrete to
build a sidewalk around the
Earth twice!

CHAPTER 4:

The Future: Being like Water

Hydropower is one of the oldest forms of renewable energy and will continue to play an important role in the future. In 1965, it produced 98% of all renewable electricity. By 2023, it still made up almost half, though solar and wind are growing fast.

Bruce Usher, who wrote *Renewable Energy: A Primer for the Twenty-first Century*, says that "the potential of hydro in the future is limited." Most big rivers already have dams, and he believes hydropower is "fully mature" in 159 countries, meaning there aren't many new places left to build. But some experts disagree. Stanford professor Mark Jacobson says hydropower will shrink in some areas because of climate change, but overall, it will grow as more places adopt it. New technology may also make

The Hetch Hetchy hydropower system helps provides electricity to the San Francisco Bay Area.

hydropower more useful, though building new dams will still be controversial because of environmental concerns.

Hydropower has many advantages—it's cheap and creates almost no pollution. But it also has downsides. Climate change can cause droughts that make hydropower less reliable. In 2018, low water levels forced some countries to switch back to fossil fuels. If dams aren't maintained well, rotting plants in the water can release methane, a powerful **greenhouse gas**. Dams can also harm wildlife, and some have led to extinctions.

Some experts, like ecologist Timothy J. Killeen, say we should remove or redesign old dams that are no longer useful or cause too much harm. One debate in the U.S. is about dams on the Columbia and Snake Rivers in Washington. Conservationists say these dams block fish like salmon from reaching their breeding grounds, while business groups argue they help shipping and provide electricity.

While Europe already has many hydroelectric dams, there is still room for growth in Asia, the Americas, and Africa. Oxford professor Nick Jelley estimates that in 2015, only a quarter of the world's hydropower potential had been built. He predicts that by 2050, hydropower production could double. One massive project, the Grand Inga dam in the Democratic Republic of the Congo, has been planned for years. If built, it would be

ZOOM IN: OLD DAMS, NEW POWER

Dam construction in the U.S. has slowed, but there's still a big opportunity to upgrade old dams. Out of 80,000 dams nationwide, only about 2,500 produce power. Most of the others are over 60 years old and need repairs. Adding hydropower to these sites could generate a lot of new electricity.

The biggest challenge ahead may be finding enough engineers to maintain and improve these dams as older workers retire. If you're considering a college major, civil engineering could be a smart choice.

ZOOM IN: HEAT FROM THE OCEAN

Ocean thermal energy conversion (OTEC)is another way to create energy in the future. it uses the difference in temperature between warm surface water and cold deep water to create power. The warm water heats up a special liquid in a pipe. The liquid turns into steam, which powers a turbine to create electricity. The liquid cools back down in the deep ocean and the process starts again.

the world's largest dam, twice as powerful as China's Three Gorges Dam. It could provide energy to millions in the region. But political instability has delayed the project, and in 2025, its main Chinese investors pulled out, making its future uncertain.

Even as traditional hydropower faces challenges, other water-based energy sources could help. Oceans cover 70% of the Earth, making them a huge potential power source. However, harnessing that energy is still a major challenge. In 2024, the U.S. Department of Energy estimated that wave power alone could generate up to 60% of America's electricity needs.

Ocean energy comes from two main sources: wave power and tidal power. Hydropower in rivers works by capturing the energy of flowing water. Tidal power works similarly but relies on the ocean's tides, which rise and fall twice a day. Wave power, on the other hand, comes from wind pushing across the ocean, creating waves. Since water is much denser than air, waves hold a lot of energy—possibly even more than wind power. However, ocean water moves unpredictably due to winds and storms, making it hard to design a system that reliably turns wave motion into electricity. Many wave power projects have been tested, but none have made it past early development. Science

The Rance Tidal Barrage, located in Brittany, France, is the world's first tidal power station,

journalist Bob McDonald points out that the ocean is a "hostile environment," and devices built for it are expensive to maintain.

Wave power devices sit on or near the ocean's surface and generate power as waves move them. Countries like Denmark, Finland, Portugal, and the U.S. have built experimental wave power projects, but none have yet become widely used. Despite the difficulties, many experts believe wave energy has great potential and could one day produce more power than wind or solar.

Tidal power doesn't rely on the wind and comes from the pull of the moon's gravity. As the Moon orbits Earth, it moves massive amounts of ocean water, creating high and low tides. These tides are predictable, unlike wind or waves, since we can track the Moon's movement far into the future. Some tidal currents are so strong they even push up rivers far from the ocean, like the Potomac River near Washington, D.C.

One way to capture tidal energy is by using a "tidal barrage." This is a dam built across an estuary, where a river meets the sea. The dam stores water at high tide and releases it through turbines to make electricity. Tidal barrages have existed since medieval times. One of the oldest modern tidal plants, the Rance Tidal Power Station in France, was built in 1966. The largest today is at Sihwa Lake in South Korea. Though much smaller than major hydro dams like

Three Gorges, they are still the biggest ocean energy projects. Right now, France and South Korea produce 90% of the world's tidal and wave energy.

Another tidal energy method, called "tidal stream," uses underwater turbines to capture energy from ocean currents. These turbines look like windmills or giant underwater kites. In Scotland, a project called MeyGen powered 4,000 homes in 2019 and is expanding to generate much more electricity. Some tidal kites are as large as airplanes, with wings up to 12 meters long. A Swedish company, Minesto, built a tidal kite that moves through underwater currents like a real kite in the wind. Since 2022, Minesto's device has been supplying power to the Faroe Islands in the North Atlantic.

Despite advancements like those seen with Minesto, some experts argue that hydropower may face more limited growth potential relative to solar and wind power in the coming decades. But it is nonetheless a versatile and economical way to create energy. Completely moving away from fossil fuels would be difficult without hydropower. As the world faces new energy challenges, adapting will be key. As Bruce Lee famously said, we must "be like water." When it comes to renewable energy and new unknowns, this may be the best advice of all.

Getting Real:

TURBINES AT WORK

Generating electricity is all about converting one kind of energy into another. Solar panels use photovoltaic cells to convert sunlight into electricity. Other forms of energy, including geothermal, wind, and hydropower, use the force of flowing liquid or air to turn machines called turbines. A windmill is a familiar example of a turbine, a machine with a rotor that turns when a fluid (such as air, steam, or water) is forced through it. This creates kinetic energy, the energy of motion. The turning turbine is attached to the rotating shaft of an electrical generator, which creates a magnetic field in a series of wire coils inside the generator, which in turn forms an electrical current. Most of the world's electricity is generated this way. Turbine systems differ in how the turbine is turned. Water and wind power push directly on the turbine, while geothermal and nuclear devices boil steam to move the turbine indirectly. Hydropower uses two main types of turbine. Reaction turbines, the most common, go directly in a stream or river and use the force of moving water to generate power. Impulse turbines use the energy from water dropping from a height, such as at a waterfall. Hydropower, of course, was used for centuries before electric power was invented—those older systems often used Ferris wheel-like machines known as waterwheels, which were perfect for agriculture or early industrial needs but generally are not powerful enough for electrical generation.

SMALL HYDRO, BIG POTENTIAL

The sheer scale and size of hydropower installations like Hoover Dam are awe-inspiring. But hydropower technology works well on a small scale too. Professor Nick Jenkins of Cardiff University says that smaller hydro plants of less than 10 megawatts in capacity often have fewer social and environmental consequences than large dams, and are becoming more popular worldwide. Some smaller installations, known as microhydropower, make 10 to 100 kilowatts of power, enough for a single house or small farm. These systems are often found in mountainous areas like the Andes and Himalayas, or hilly regions in China or the Philippines. The type of turbines used in huge dams like Three Gorges usually are too costly and complex for microhydropower, and simpler devices like impulse turbines generally get better results. Options include Pelton or Turgo wheels, which work by funneling high-pressure water into a spray jet that turns a turbine; the low-power Jack Rabbit turbine, which works in streams that are only 13 inches deep; and a Garman turbine, which looks a bit like an airplane propellor. Microhydropower could be an excellent solution for rural areas not connected to a nationwide grid, especially remote villages near fast-flowing streams. But the technology is still expensive and has not yet been perfected for wide use. Like a lot of alternative-energy installations, microhydropower might work best as part of a larger system of power generation—in particular, microhydropower would work well with solar power, since the two are each strongest in different seasons.

Timeline

3rd century BCE

Ancient Egyptians use Archimedes' water screws for irrigation.

1770s

French engineer Bernard Forest de Bélidor writes *Architecture Hydraulique*, describing early hydropower machines

1880

The first hydroelectric power plant in Grand Rapids, Michigan, generates electricity for arc lighting

1882

World's first central DC hydroelectric station powers a paper mill in Appleton, Wisconsin.

1895

Niagara Falls hydropower station begins operation.

1902

The U.S. Reclamation Act establishes the Bureau of Reclamation to manage water resources and build hydropower plants.

1930s

Construction of iconic dams like Hoover Dam and Grand Coulee Dam under the U.S. New Deal.

1940s–1970s

Rapid expansion of hydropower facilities worldwide, driven by post-war growth.

1966

The Rance Tidal Barrage in France becomes the world's first tidal power station.

21st century

Hydropower evolves with innovations in marine energy.

Websites

INTERNATIONAL HYDROPOWER ASSOCIATION
https://www.hydropower.org/
The website of this nonprofit organization representing 120 countries features facts and videos about hydropower around the world.

HOOVER DAM
https://www.usbr.gov/lc/hooverdam/
Run by the U.S. Bureau of Reclamation, the official website of this historic dam has a wealth of photos and articles about its construction and operation.

ENERGY KIDS: HYDROPOWER
https://www.eia.gov/kids/energy-sources/hydropower/
This U.S. Energy Information Administration website is a fun resource for more information about hydroelectricity.

Glossary

dam - a barrier constructed across a river to block its water flow

flow - A measure of the volume of water going through an area over a given time

fossil fuel -hydrocarbon fuels such as petroleum oil and gas made in the ancient past from biological sources and found in Earth's crust

greenhouse gas - gases such as carbon dioxide, methane, and water vapor which contribute to global warming by absorbing infrared radiation (heat) and reflecting it back to Earth's surface

global warming - a human-caused increase in worldwide air and ocean temperature

gravity - the physical force of attraction which causes water to flow from high to low elevation

head: the height difference between where water enters and leaves a hydropower facility, which increases the amount of power the water generates

hydraulic: operated or moved by the force of water

hydropower: the use of moving or falling water to create power; when used specifically to make electricity, it is known as hydroelectricity

irrigation: the process of bringing water to dry regions to aid farming

renewability: a goal for alternative energy that it will never run out (such as sunlight and wind) or will replenish over time.

reservoir: a manmade body of water, often created by a dam

sustainability: a goal for alternative energy that it will not damage Earth's climate or humans' ability to harvest it.

water cycle: the natural process in which water evaporates into the atmosphere, falls as rain and returns through rivers to the ocean

waterwheel: a wheel driven by flowing water to power machinery

Selected Bibliography

Berners-Lee, Mike. *There Is No Planet B: A Handbook for the Make Or Break Years*. United States, Cambridge University Press, 2019.

Jacobson, Mark Z.. *No Miracles Needed: How Today's Technology Can Save Our Climate and Clean Our Air*. United Kingdom, Cambridge University Press, 2023.

Jelley, Nick. *Renewable Energy: A Very Short Introduction*. United Kingdom, OUP Oxford, 2020.

Jenkins, Nick. *Energy Systems: A Very Short Introduction*. United Kingdom, Oxford University Press, 2019.

Killeen, Timothy J., *A Perfect Storm in the Amazon Wilderness: Success and Failure in the Fight to Save an Ecosystem of Critical Importance to the Planet*. United Kingdom: White Horse Press, 2021.

McDonald, Bob. *The Future Is Now: Solving the Climate Crisis with Today's Technologies*. Canada, Penguin Canada, 2024.

Meier, Paul F., *The Changing Energy Mix: A Systematic Comparison of Renewable and Nonrenewable Energy* (New York, 2020; online edn, Oxford Academic, 18 Feb. 2021),

Rhodes, Richard. *Energy: A Human History*. United Kingdom: Simon & Schuster, 2019.

Ritter, Bill. *Powering Forward: What Everyone Should Know About America's Energy Revolution*. United States, Fulcrum Publishing, 2016.

Index